the parent-child emotional impasses usually associated with power struggles in parent-child relationships. Parents are empowered to aim for understanding, but not in an 'intellectualized,' cerebral sense.

Through many illustrations, the book brings together the two generations, children and adults, searching for the overlapping elements in the history of and repetitions of anger-provoking situations. The best and worst of the parents' emotional experiences with their own parents are reflected on, as Dr. Hollman suggests, which can produce empathy and constructive options in the present moment.

This book incorporates psychodynamic principles and practical wisdom for learning from our children and adolescent's angry experiences. Parents can learn new approaches at problem solving from the perspective of child and family development and meaning-making. It's like having Dr. Hollman as a live-in psychological-expert childminder. Read the book twice!"

—CARL BAGNINI, LCSW, BCD

Senior faculty, International Psychotherapy Institute, Washington, DC and Long Island, NY teaching child and family therapy, couple therapy and psychoanalytic supervision

"In her excellent book *Unlocking Parental Intelligence: Finding Meaning in Your Child's Behavior*, Dr. Hollman encouraged parents to seek out the meaning of their child or teen's misbehavior before trying to deal with it. She showed parents how to pause and reflect on their thoughts and feelings about the situation and how to think about their child's possibly different thoughts and feelings and his or her developmental level. She explained how understanding the meaning of their child's behavior enables parents to empathically resolve problem behaviors.

This new book is a superb follow-up that provides a short, practical guide for parents struggling to manage their child or teen's angry behavior. Dr. Hollman summarizes the Parental Intelligence principles and gives insightful real-world examples of the principles in action with angry children. The book is a quick, easy read that offers real help for managing different kinds of anger in children and teens. Highly recommended."

—JANET WILDE ASTINGTON, PHD

Professor Emeritus. Institute of Child Study, Department of Human Development and Applied Psychology, University of Toronto; Editor, *Minds in the Making*

"Dr. Hollman builds upon the approach contained in her first book, *Unlocking Parental Intelligence: Finding Meaning in Your Child's Behavior* by focusing on children's anger. Her empathic and self-reflective method is illustrated in various vignettes and accompanied by practical tips that provide parents with valuable tools to facilitate development of self-regulation, insight, and problem-solving skills in themselves and their children while building stronger and more satisfying family bonds. This book will appeal to all parents committed to raising their children into thoughtful and emotionally intelligent adults and future parents. Highly recommended for educators, policy makers, and therapists as well."

—LYNN SESKIN, PSYD

Clinical and School Psychologist

"Children's anger is a significant challenge for parents to deal with. Dr. Laurie Hollman's book provides parents with an insightful approach to responding to their children's anger through understanding their children's actions as well as reflecting on their own reactions. She illustrates her approach with clear examples of working out problems with children. This book should enable parents to help their children deal with anger and enjoy their children even more."

—JEREMY CARPENDALE, PHD

Professor of Developmental Psychology, Department of Psychology,
Simon Fraser University, Burnaby, BC V5A 1S6 Canada

The BUSY PARENT'S GUIDE to MANAGING ANGER IN CHILDREN AND TEENS

THE PARENTAL INTELLIGENCE WAY

FAMILIUS

Copyright © 2018 by Laurie Hollman

Published by Familius LLC, www.familius.com

Familius books are available at special discounts for bulk purchases, whether for sales promotions or for family or corporate use. For more information, contact Familius Sales at 559-876-2170 or email orders@familius.com.

Library of Congress Cataloging-in-Publication Data
2018934006

Print ISBN 9781641700115
Ebook ISBN 9781641700566

Printed in the United States of America

Edited by Brooke Jorden
Cover design by David Miles
Book design by Brooke Jorden

10 9 8 7 6 5 4 3 2 1
First Edition

LAURIE HOLLMAN, PhD

The BUSY PARENT'S GUIDE to MANAGING ANGER IN CHILDREN AND TEENS

A QUICK READ FOR POWERFUL SOLUTIONS!

THE PARENTAL INTELLIGENCE WAY

To Jeff, for his loving empathy and compassion as a husband and father.

ACKNOWLEDGMENTS

I am thankful for all those who have inspired and helped me with this book. First and foremost, I am grateful to my husband, Jeff, my partner in life, for his unending support of my ongoing writing about parenting. He has always strengthened my resolve to put my ideas into words. My gratitude also goes to my sons, David and Rich, who were raised with Parental Intelligence and continue to discuss my concepts and support their evolution. I would also like to thank Claire, David's wife, my wonderful daughter-in-law, for her continual enthusiasm and encouragement of my work.

With pleasure, I give thanks to the delightful staff at Familius for publishing my books, including founder and president Christopher Robbins, who supports his authors so well, and David Miles for his artistic book covers.

Particularly at Familius, I am appreciative of my gifted editor, Brooke Jorden, whose devotion to her work and expertise as a writer has enhanced my book and brought it to fruition. I am further grateful to Leah Welker, who also edited this book with talent and effectiveness.

In addition, I thank the many parents and their children and adolescents in my practice over the years who inspired my desire to write this book, so others could benefit from their courage in building strong parent-child and parent-adolescent ties.

As my psychoanalytic training and research has progressed throughout the many years of my practice, I am grateful to the voices of so many others who have influenced me and broadened and deepened my psychological knowledge.

I conclude by thanking my loving grandsons—Zander, age 9, and Eddie, age 7, at the time I wrote this book—for their impressive insights into how children think and feel. Their wondrous ability to put their ideas into words supports and inspires my belief in young children's capacities to be empathic and capable problem solvers. When they confide in me their personal thoughts and wishes, I am reminded of the essence of Parental Intelligence: the close bonds it brings between parent and child, grandparent and grandchild.

CONTENTS

INTRODUCTION

Do you wonder why your child or teen seems on edge, unduly angry, and restless at times—or maybe all the time? Are you uncertain if and when you should be worried? Are you so busy that sometimes you dismiss these thoughts but later reconsider them? You may be noticing you have a frequently angry child or teen.

Ever since I wrote the book, *Unlocking Parental Intelligence: Finding Meaning in Your Child's Behavior*, parents and professionals have requested I write some short practical books on the challenges parents face, such as managing anger in their kids. In my psychotherapy practice, I have seen that anger is a difficult state of mind, but with guidance, parents can help their children understand, manage, modify, and even master their anger. This book hopes to address those challenges to help you, the parent, understand and manage the behavior and feelings of children and teens with both fleeting and frequent anger.

It's important to distinguish the wide gradations in anger—from minor annoyance to frustration, fury, and rage—and how well your child can control each level of anger. After due consideration of the causes, it is healthy to assert one's anger in a controlled and directed way. Expressing feelings of anger can be a reasonable assertion of one's point of view, beliefs, intentions, and motivations and can lead to productive dialogue. Using Parental Intelligence, which will be described in this book, you can help your children and teens to understand and express angry feelings with self-confidence and positive outcomes that lead to resolutions of varied problems. Parental Intelligence is an approach to parenting that helps busy parents like you have an organized way to attend to these varied situations, whether they are minimal or excessive.

It's common to suffer along with your angry child and feel parenting is beyond you, as if it requires a special kind of intelligence that wasn't encrypted on your brain. I've been inspired to write this book after thirty years as a psychoanalyst working with mothers and fathers who came to me at different stages in their parenting careers, questioning how to help their angry kids. They were all searching for that special intelligence needed for such parenting, even if they didn't quite know how to ask for it.

I coined the term *Parental Intelligence* because I believe parents who are willing to pause and reflect before they react can find many of the answers and insights they need within themselves. Parenting angry kids requires special tools that give you a new perspective on anger that enlightens, uplifts, and relieves you as you learn how to discover the meaning behind this distressing emotional response. As you continue to practice this process, you will become a *meaning-maker*, empowered to read the thoughts and feelings underlying your child's anger like an open book. You will come to understand that anger is an emotional state that expresses or communicates meaningful thoughts and feelings that you can learn to decipher. Once you understand what is going through your child's or teen's mind, you can collaborate with him or her to solve problems. This not only relieves anger but also strengthens the parent-child bond.

Angry feelings vary from each other in the types of situations that produce these emotions, the subsequent behaviors, and the associated thoughts that accompany

these feelings. With Parental Intelligence, you will figure out the *whys* behind your child's angry responses.
With Parental Intelligence, you enter the inner world
of your child or teen and understand where he or she
is coming from. As you try to calm your upset child or
teen, you will not only focus on relieving the anger in
the moment, but also in the long run. To do so, you will
realize you first need to understand the meaning behind
the anger and even consider it a useful communication
and an invitation to empathic understanding.

In this book, I am going to describe the five steps
to Parental Intelligence that provide the tools you will
need to approach anger in your child or teen using
multiple examples. I will offer specific suggestions on
how to help your kids cope with angry states of mind
and understand the meanings behind these complex
emotional experiences. It is my hope that the straight-
forward information provided in this book will help
prevent anger from escalating and offer reassurance
when you feel uncertain, giving you the pleasure of
helping your child or teen grow and develop.

The chapters are arranged to explain and illustrate
various situations that give rise to anger: when kids say
"No"; when parents say "No"; temper tantrums, and
anger resulting from interpersonal situations. I will
describe the key features of each instance of anger for
kids of various ages.

I have written fictionalized accounts of anger in children and adolescents and associated family dynamics to preserve the privacy of my patients and people I've come across in daily life. These stories demonstrate how each angry situation can be managed and resolved using Parental Intelligence, and the result is a closer parent-child bond and greater overall understanding. Parental Intelligence not only provides the busy parent a structured approach to helping angry kids, but also a vision of hope: an avenue for parents to better understand their children at all ages and developmental levels. Using Parental Intelligence, parents support their angry kids as they help them solve their problems and lead loving, satisfying lives.

CHAPTER ONE

THE PARENTAL INTELLIGENCE WAY

*An angry reaction carries a message.
It is an invitation for understanding.*

While each parent faces unique challenges, I have discovered many commonalities that affect varied situations. To help you parent effectively, I have developed five powerfully valuable steps that will allow you—no matter how different your circumstances may be or how busy you are—to find meaning behind your child or teen's anger and, beyond that, to intelligently and compassionately resolve the underlying problems.

The five steps to Parental Intelligence are:

1. Stepping Back
2. Self-Reflecting
3. Understanding Your Child's Mind
4. Understanding Your Child's Development
5. Problem Solving

Together, these five steps provide a road map to help you get to your destination: the place where you understand the meaning behind your child or teen's anger. What was obscure becomes clear. When meanings are understood, it's easier to decide the best ways to handle the situation. As new information comes to light, empathy between you and your child will deepen. (*Child* refers to your son or daughter at any age, from toddler to teenager.) Going through the five-step process with your child or teen uncovers problems of greater significance than the original anger suggested and a stronger alliance forms between you and your child.

STEP ONE
Stepping Back

A parent's first reactions to a child or teen's anger is often emotional. Without distance from these emotions, you might make rash decisions that do not achieve desired results and that you will regret later. Responding effectively means starting from that uncomfortable emotional place but making it a priority to step back, tolerate the child or teen's feelings, and gradually shift to a more reasoned response leading to a better outcome the first time around rather than after multiple instances of trial and error. This is what a busy parent wants and needs: a method they can trust and fall back on automatically that offers their child more understanding and coping mechanisms.

Imagine a video of an angry reaction played back in slow motion to get a detailed picture of what occurred. Track the anger, giving it a beginning, middle, and end. This allows you to recall what happened before the incident—what your child did, what you did, and how you felt—and sets the stage for future, more enlightened parenting choices.

Stepping back requires opening up your thinking and allowing yourself to experience a range of emotions without taking immediate action. Sometimes, after an angry incident, parents feel anxious, on edge, and restless and will immediately jump into action to alleviate these feelings. Other times, parents refrain from acting impulsively but feel a nagging tension—a need to *act*—that interferes with their ability to see the situation objectively. Such a parent may be stuck in one point of view or focus solely on a specific but incomplete set of details.

If you never pause, you never allow emotions to subside and thinking to begin. The process of stepping back allows you to suspend judgment and give yourself time to figure out what happened before taking action. Stepping back prepares you to engage in the parenting mindset that says what happened is meaningful. Even in an emergency, once the immediate situation has been handled, there is room for refraining from ready conclusions and for stepping back. You may feel reluctant to look inside, to experience emotions, for fear of feeling out of control, but in order to respond to your child's anger, it is essential—especially if you want your child or teen to learn how to gain control themselves.

Stepping back requires suspending judgment not only about your child's anger, but also about your parenting behavior. Stepping back gives you permission to not always know what to do. Consequently, when a parent reacts one way on the spot, but later understands what happened more fully, he or she can feel confident returning to the child with new thoughts and feelings that have begun to expand, offering new perspectives.

When you step back, you recognize anger can have many causes. By pausing, you give yourself time to compare the last time you encountered your child's angry outburst to the present or a similar situation. You discover a pattern in your parent-child interaction and wonder, *Are there many causes for this anger I couldn't consider at the time? What triggered the anger? How long did it last? When did it escalate or decrease?* You start to see facets you were blind to because of your child's and your own high emotional states during the incident.

Once you're in the mode of seeking full knowledge of what happened, you will begin to discover that multiple factors might be involved in one angry reaction by your child or teen. Calmer, you notice expressions on your child's face and their tone of voice, gestures, postures, mood, and shifts in feelings. After a while, this one situation can be understood as having multiple causes.

Stepping back gives you time to evaluate the situation, examine and question assumptions, and realize there is more beneath the surface you still need to understand. Take as much time as you need to consider what is happening. Say to yourself, *Slo-o-o-w down. Take your time. Hold on. Resist those impulses. Breathe deeply. Sit quietly. Consider what to say or do, if anything.*

When you give yourself permission to slow down before reacting, you reduce stress and feel more in control. The tenor changes between you and your child. When kids see parents taking their time, they start to feel, perhaps cautiously at first, that their parents can be trusted to guide them. The busy parent's calm is already effective in building that relationship of trust that will be necessary for eventual problem solving.

Stepping back requires tolerating frustration—a skill we want to teach our angry children. While thinking over what occurred, acknowledge that anger carries meaning. This parenting approach accepts that angry reactions communicate deeper motives. Sometimes, it may indicate problems that need to be solved in the parent-child relationship. The next step, self-reflecting, increases parents' abilities to understand their own feelings and motives that led to their actions.

STEP TWO
Self-Reflecting

Self-reflecting helps you discover how your past affects your present approach to parenting. Self-reflecting allows you to observe yourself objectively and think about the genesis of your feelings, motives, and actions in both present and previous relationships. This step requires questioning why you behaved the way you did. I know it can be hard. It's so tempting to just jump to offering solutions to your child and skip questioning what's going on inside of *you*, especially when you're busy. But it actually takes less time in the long run than trying many approaches that continually fail.

For parents, self-reflecting is an extension of stepping back. It requires considering what led to your responses to your child's anger, prompts you to think about your actions from many perspectives, and allows you to consider many causes for your responses.

You question, *Why did I react that particular way, now that I see it wasn't the only way? What were my motives and intentions? What in my past affected my thinking and actions in the present? What were my emotional reactions to my child's anger, and where did they come from?* Self-reflecting is a discovery process. Knowing yourself better, you feel more confident. It feels good to learn about yourself and the effect your experiences had on your present reactions to your child.

Self-reflecting often leads to a realization that you take your child's anger personally. While hard to accept, it's also relieving to understand. Sometimes you feel persecuted by your child; you want to be the boss, yet your child seems to have control. If you reflect further and consider how to be authoritative, yet kind and compassionate, you will feel better about yourself.

Think of your child's distress and your feelings during the incident. Now find a past experience that triggered similar feelings. Review it slowly, like a story, in as much detail as you can. Think about the people in your life at that time and what they meant to you. You may find your child's present feelings trigger aspects from that past situation. Ask yourself: *Does my child's anger remind me of my angry reactions in the past? Does my child remind me of someone else's anger in the past?* These memories may have to do with the way you now react to your child.

There are several possibilities. If your child's behavior, manner, posture, or tone of voice resonate with how you interacted with someone else at earlier times in your life, you may be reacting to your child the way you reacted when you were younger. Alternatively, it may be someone was angry at you the way your child is now, and that is what's so upsetting to you. Past and present have converged. No wonder you reacted so strongly.

Flexible, sensitized decision-making comes to bear on the situation. Insight builds bridges to your child that lead to understanding your child's mind—step three in this parenting approach.

STEP THREE
Understanding Your Child's Mind

"What's on your mind?" is a question often asked casually, but central to knowing your child or teen. Understanding your child's mind starts with knowing your child's mental states and experiences: their intentions, thoughts, desires, beliefs, and feelings.

Your ability to understand your child's mind is directly related to your ability to self-reflect. As described above, self-reflecting is your capacity to think about your own experiences. When, with self-reflecting, you are able to understand how your own mind is working, you also realize your child's mind is separate and autonomous from yours. However, if you do not understand this, you may unknowingly attribute your own mental states (intentions and feelings) to your child.

For example, let's say you're upset at your ten-year-old for being curt with you after you made a delicious breakfast of toast with jam, granola, and his favorite fruit-juice smoothie—the works! However, he barely says, "Good morning," grabs the toast, and runs out the door. You feel disrespected. He barely noticed what you'd done. You assume he's mad at you from his quick, "See ya," with his back toward you. In your mind, he was angry at you and the anger was unjustified. The assumption is simple: you're angry; he's angry. You've forgotten that your child's feelings and intentions may be quite different from your own. In this example, what actually happened, you find out later, was your child was curt because he was late for the school bus. He was in a hurry. He wasn't mad at you at all.

Here's another example. A teen, just home from a demanding lacrosse game, is frustrated when dinner service is slow at a restaurant. He angrily protests that he's starving instead of containing himself. His father had a big lunch, is enjoying everyone's company, and doesn't mind waiting. He finds his fifteen-year-old's complaints rude. He berates and humiliates him in front of everyone, telling him to be silent the rest of the meal or he can't go out later. The son feels embarrassed, resentful, and angry. Their mental states—their intentions and feelings—are different. His father mistakenly assumed that what is on his mind should also be on his son's mind.

Such inability to be aware that one's own mental state is different from that of one's child can lead a parent to misinterpret the intent of the child's anger, causing a rupture in the parent-child relationship. Understanding your child's mind depends on realizing the links between intentions, feelings, thoughts, and behaviors and looking for the meanings behind angry reactions.

Alternatively, a self-reflective mother might say to her son, "You punched the wall when your brother took your baseball mitt without asking. He's been doing this for weeks, and your frustration has reached its limit. Think about it. Could it be that by hitting the wall, you were avoiding hitting him?" Now that she's planted a new idea in her son's mind, she continues, "Let's think and talk more about your frustration so you don't ever need to punch a wall." She's now connected his emotions (anger and frustration) to his behavior (punching).

A parent who approaches the situation this way is attuned to what's going on in her child's mind that caused the angry behavior. While the father in the restaurant above was unable to shift to understanding his son's mind, this mother linked her son's internal emotional state to his external behavior. She used Parental Intelligence—so essential for the busy parent who wants a strong relationship with her child.

Anger is meaningful, even if you don't catch on to the specific meaning right away. You need to let the emotions sit in your mind. This shows empathy: "It seems like your feelings were hurt by the teacher so you angrily bolted out of the classroom. Was it something like that?" Your child confirms she was feeling hurt, and you continue, "Now that we can figure out what was going on in your mind, were there other choices you may have had, so you can react another way next time you feel angry and hurt?" Again, Parental Intelligence at work.

No one likes being told how they should feel, but it sure feels good to be understood. Everyone appreciates empathy. Feeling understood can help a child contain her emotions and begin to think them through. When a child feels her parent understands what is going on inside her mind, she feels supported and can think further about how to handle situations.

Understanding your child's mind is part of empathy—understanding the emotional states of another. It's like trying to step into your child's shoes and see from his point of view. However, no one can know another person's mind with complete accuracy. Thus, it's often best to approach the task by asking questions rather than by making statements. You'll feel great when your son or daughter says, "You really get it. Thanks."

To understand your child's mind, it helps to be a good observer. Verbal communication is only one piece of the puzzle. Speech, of course, helps us understand the other's mind, but silence, stiffening or relaxation of muscles, and facial expressions reveal various emotions. Watch your child's facial expressions to get an idea of what's on her mind. Here are examples described by Paul Ekman in his book *Emotions Revealed*: a furrowed brow may communicate worry or anger, crinkled lines at the edges of eyes may indicate anger, and a wrinkled nose may communicate annoyance. Finger pointing, averting her head, turning her back, folding her arms, or standing and storming away often suggest anger. Remember that every child will have unique facial expressions and reactions. The better you know your child, the better you will be at interpreting your observations.

Sometimes we are blind to anger in our children that we block out in ourselves. For instance, a hurt parent who blocks out her own anger may be blind to her child's anger. Parents might believe they or their child or teen feels only one emotion (hurt) while truly feeling something else (anger). If this is true, then recognizing your child's anger and more hidden hurt might lead to you feel your own. If you don't know what is on your own mind—what you are thinking and feeling—you may subsequently be blocked from understanding what is on your child's mind—what he or she is thinking and feeling—and draw erroneous conclusions.

Parents who are able to think about their children's minds manage their parent-child relationships better and are more effective in resolving inevitable conflicts and arguments. It shows kids you believe in them and teaches them to believe in themselves. Treating your children and adolescents like capable human beings with well-functioning minds and good intentions builds their confidence and trust.

STEP FOUR
Understanding Your Child's Development

There are developmental stages when children and teenagers master different skills, but not all youngsters reach those stages at the same time. Your seven-year-old may be more adept at math than your nine-year-old. Your thirteen-year-old may be more empathic than your sixteen-year-old.

The age when a child reaches a certain skill level is the child's *developmental age* for that skill, regardless of the child's chronological age. When parents take into account the developmental age of their child—the stage the child has reached in mastering certain capacities—parents and children get along better.

What capacities should you look for? Notice your child's interpersonal skills: impulse control, effective communication, and empathy. Watch for the development of autonomy, identity formation, and self-reliance. Children aren't consistent across the board; they each have their own strengths and weaknesses. Their chronological age may not be the same as their developmental age for any of these capacities, and children may be at different developmental levels for different skills. When you set expectations for your children, be sure they reflect developmental levels, which may fall behind or step ahead of their chronological age. Healthcare providers such as pediatricians discuss child development at yearly check-ups. Teachers, social workers, and psychologists also discuss child development in parent conferences in schools. These interventions keep the parent in tune with what to expect for their particular child.

Ask two questions: "What is expected at my child's stage of development?" and "How far apart is my child's chronological age from my child's developmental age?" Being critical of a child for not completing tasks only expected for a chronological age creates problems that affect your relationship. Expectations that do not reflect your child's developmental age won't be met and will create emotional distress, frustration, and even anger. This is especially true for a child with delays that prevent him from reaching the milestones of that age.

Once you have stepped back, self-reflected, and understood your child's mind, understanding your child's developmental stage becomes essential for effective problem solving.

STEP FIVE
Problem Solving

The more you continue working on these steps, the more natural they will become, preparing you for the last step: problem solving. Interestingly, by now, the initial problem—the specific angry reaction—has become part of a set of problems to be solved over time. The immediate importance of the initial anger may have lessened because you have recognized it as a symptom of more pressing underlying issues. These are the problems you ultimately hope to solve, together with your child, using Parental Intelligence.

Problem solving aims to find meanings which may be new to both participants. Take turns talking things out to correct misinterpretations and seek meanings behind the anger in question. This approach saves a lot of time for busy folks. Parent and child learn new coping skills that can be used in the future.

While problem solving, you reflect on your view and your child's view of reality. If you and your child can see the problem from each other's points of view, you can problem solve together.

The steps leading from stepping back to problem solving seem linear, but you may need to go back and forth among them. If, for example, you consider the anger at hand to be intentionally antagonistic behavior (see chapters 3 and 4) or an ensuing power conflict, then it is important to go back to earlier steps.

Or if, during problem solving, you find your child's voice is tinged with sarcasm, you may be off track. Perhaps a new problem has surfaced, signaled by the sarcasm. Address that issue first, and use your new skills (e.g., understanding your child's mind) to identify what is driving your child to speak that way to you. Reflect on potential triggers. In each of these instances, taking a break from problem solving to figure out your own and your child's reactions will be well worth the effort.

Becoming a meaning-maker with regard to the causes of anger is a profound experience that can change how you view your children, your teens, and yourself. Busy parents need this organized approach, rather than trial-and-error parenting that actually takes more time. Unlocking Parental Intelligence introduces a new stage of parenting life that will have long-lasting results in how family members engage each other, care for each other, and view and solve problems.

CHAPTER TWO

HEALTHY EXPRESSIONS
OF ANGER

*A*ngry feelings are natural for kids—and adults, for that matter—for all kinds of reasons. It's healthy for parents to give the impression that emotions are normal and everyone has them. To do this early on, teach young kids feeling language, like *happy, sad, mad,* and *glad.* Then, as they grow older, give them the nuances of anger, such as *irritated, frustrated, disappointed, annoyed, hurt, livid, heated,* and *enraged.* This vocabulary is important if the child is to assess how angry they actually feel and why.

Naming the emotions this way gives kids the opportunity to express themselves in words rather than physical actions when they are upset. It's our job as parents with Parental Intelligence to listen carefully, without arguing your kids' points at first, to really try and understand what is distressing them. If children and teens feel their parent is willing to step back and listen to their emotions, particularly anger, they can experience these feelings without being fearful of themselves for having angry feelings—or being fearful of their parents' reactions while expressing them.

Anger is not only unavoidable, but also a form of expressing oneself as a person. At times in a child's and teen's development, anger is a way of establishing his independence. In this book, you will learn how to help your child or teen grow up feeling confident and independent, yet safe in their outbursts by establishing limits that help them feel in control of their emotions.

Listening to angry feelings is difficult—especially if they are directed at you! No one likes to feel someone is mad at them. But the overriding issue to keep in mind, even when you are busy, is that because we love and care for our youngsters, we need to know what upsets them so we can discover whatever is problematic and hopefully help them reach some resolutions.

It's important you tolerate angry feelings and not try to dissuade your child or teen from having these feelings at all. Your child or teen should not feel that you are afraid of these feelings or that you will judge him harshly for having them. Kids need to know that having and expressing anger doesn't make them a bad person.

It's also important for kids to know that their anger doesn't make them too powerful for their parents to hear and endure. Experiencing anger can actually frighten kids, and they need to know that having and expressing such emotions doesn't frighten their parents, too. Then they won't be scared to share these feelings with you. It may be an adjustment to realize your children fear their own anger, but it can overwhelm them, which is why they need to express it and understand it with your guidance. If you can allow for such distress, then your child or teen knows she can trust you to remain stable while she expresses these feelings and that you will help her work them out. When busy parents remain stable and calm in the face of their child's anger, it saves a lot of time in managing the anger so it can be understood.

Sometimes anger is an overreaction to something gone awry, but it's best not to tell your child or teen this right off. This kind of dismissal will make them shut down and probably shut you out, and you won't be able to help them through this maze of emotions. Instead, by listening carefully to the underlying issues, you will begin to understand their mind. This permits a discussion of different perspectives about the situation at hand. Hearing your child's points of view before you express your own (which may be similar or different) allows the youngster to feel heard and believe everyone will understand his situation further. This also saves a lot of time for a busy parent by keeping the lines of communication open.

A simple tip is to ask your child or teen to tell you more about the situation and how they feel about it. We want to stretch their capacity to express themselves and articulate their emotions before we rush in with our vantage points. The more parents and kids have healthy, helpful discussions, the more the child or teen will be able to control and regulate their angry emotions by articulating them, not only at home, but also in the world outside of our protection.

Ideally, children and teens can learn that they can tell us, their parents, about their angry feelings openly, but it's not always a good idea in the outside world to be so forthcoming. They need to learn to regard others' feelings and make sound decisions about what they say when, where, and to whom. The astute parent shares this wisdom with their child so he or she knows how to socialize confidently and reasonably.

Psychologists talk about regulating emotions. This is especially important when it comes to angry feelings.

It means the child can contain his anger and delay expressing it until it will be reasonably well received. This means the child can wait, delay, and suspend their expressions of anger using sound judgment. If they learn about this idea at home from parents who step back and self-reflect, it will help them with their peers and other adults.

In the long run, these lessons become internalized by a child only if their parent also follows these basic tenets of self-regulation. If we, as parents, too impulsively express our anger at home or outside the home when our kids are present, we won't set the example we are aiming for. When your child sees you have cause for anger but delay expressing it until you have assessed your options for articulating it, your child observes keenly how to do this for themselves.

Here's an example that didn't go well: Spouses were arguing in a room about how their finances were being managed. They were interrupting each other, raising their voices, not hearing each other's points of view. Very frustrated, the father withdrew into silence. This infuriated his wife further, and she berated him for his "usual, vengeful silent treatment." She was too angry to consider that he was silent, not out of revenge as she surmised, but because he was trying to get himself back in control. Next door, their seven-year-old was listening intently. Disturbed by the ruckus, he went to see his older fifteen-year-old brother who had also overheard his parents' usual pattern of handling each other's anger. The younger child needed his older brother's guidance and companionship. However, the older brother dismissed him and yelled, "Go away. I'm watching an R-rated movie, and you can't be here." Then, lo and behold, he gave his younger sibling the silent treatment. Crushed, the little one went back to his room alone, in tears.

For kids to internalize an ability to regulate their emotions, they need to witness their parents doing the same, contrary to the example above. This means they will watch you like a hawk when they know you are in a situation that causes you anger. They benefit from observing you delaying, waiting, and assessing the situation before determining what to say, when to say it, and to whom. Kids learn by the example you set.

Here are a few parenting tips of what not to do:

1. Don't forget that our kids hear how we handle each others' anger, even behind closed doors.
2. Don't yell at a yelling child.
3. Don't make fun of your child's anger, even if it's an overreaction.
4. Don't put in your two cents before you really hear your child out. This means stepping back and delaying your reactions until the child seems

finished communicating what's on his mind.

5. Don't walk away abruptly, dismissing your angry child and saying, "I can't listen to this now!" without setting a time when you can and do listen.

6. Don't curse in your child's presence.

And if you slip up—which, of course, we all do—point out your regret to the child and let him know how you wished you'd handled the situation. Everyone loses control sometimes, and everyone makes mistakes. This, too, is a lesson worth teaching and remembering for all concerned.

Thus, it's natural, normal, and healthy for kids to know when they feel angry. If they believe their parents believe this, they will be forthcoming with their emotions and trust that their parents can help them to manage by understanding them. To reiterate, it's essential that you allow your kids these feelings and that your kids know and understand that you can tolerate, endure, and even appreciate these emotions. If they don't get this impression from you, their anger goes underground and seeps out eventually. These suppressed feelings may resurface in behaviors, such as acting out or even withdrawing in despair, and not knowing why they feel so inhibited.

Thus, if your child knows from experience that her feelings won't cause you to become unstable, she won't worry that her feelings are too powerful for you, an adult who loves her, to hear. I emphasize this because it is an essential point to keep in mind. If kids feel their anger will knock their parents' socks off, they will be reluctant to share these emotions. They need to hear you say, "It's okay to feel angry. Tell me more about it so I can understand where you're coming from." This sentence is so relieving to a child or teen. This response alone can calm the child down quickly and effectively—a lifesaver for the busy parent.

Parents aren't perfect, as we all know so well. We make mistakes, get out of control, lose our tempers, and regret things we've said. This is inevitable, but not without remedy. It's valuable to tell your child you reacted too quickly and wish you had responded in a different way. Tell them your preferred response and go on from there. Let them know and feel you really want to get it from their point of view before pushing your vantage point on them. When a child or teen feels heard, then they are able and willing to listen as well.

Learning what happened to their youngest child after their fight over finances, the parents in the above example changed their ways while discussing the same subject the next day. The parents first admitted to each other that they blew it, not only with each other but also with their kids, setting a harmful example for how the two brothers should treat each other. This time, both parents went over their expenses, listened without interrupting each other, and then spoke angrily but quietly about what they objected to. They both expressed their fears of their income lowering and came to grips with some compromises. Both boys overheard the discussion (which the parents were aware of in this small home) and, while worried their parents were angry, they felt reassured they could resolve their differences and stay in control.

Following this second discussion amongst themselves, the parents shared with their sons that they knew the boys had overheard their previous, unsuccessful argument and they intended to communicate with each other more effectively the second time around. They wanted their kids to know they understood that listening to parents argue is distressing, but both adults and kids can redo a discussion in order to not only solve the problem at hand, but also become assured that arguments can be resolved and relationships strengthened as a result.

In effect, this family and yours can learn that anger is a normal, healthy emotion when expressed after stepping back, self-reflecting, and understanding what's going on in the other person's mind. In this way, busy mothers and fathers can use their Parental Intelligence to foster problem solving with their kids—even those problems first expressed angrily.

CHAPTER THREE

WHEN KIDS SAY "NO"

At least once a week, six-year-old Lee has trouble dealing with the normal authority of his parents. This has been going on for six months now. He frequently says "No" to his parents' requests without provocation and, from their point of view, seems to be annoying them deliberately. In Lee's mind, he says "No" to requests that are unreasonable, but even when his parents aren't making requests of him, he is easily annoyed and often angry and resentful. He blames others for his mistakes or misbehavior. Rarely, but noticeably, he seems spiteful toward his mother in particular. This behavior only occurs at home. In his first-grade class, he is compliant with his teacher's authority and, in fact, is doing well academically. He is learning how to read and write and enjoys his math and science lessons.

Lee's family at first consisted of himself as an only child with his parents, who have an argumentative marriage but without cause for alarm or even potential separation. Their disagreements surfaced most clearly when Lee's siblings were born: twin boys who are now ten months old. They now crawl actively and have even begun to stand up and hold on to things so they can roam about their small home.

Lee's temperament prior to their arrival had been somewhat difficult as he had problems tolerating frustrations. This seemed pretty normal for his age until the twins were born, when he couldn't possibly get the same attention from his mother that he was used to.

Lee's mother stays at home and his father works as an accountant, coming home about six o'clock each evening. Lee's father is the first to notice that Lee is acting in a defiant way when the twins are born. His wife is preoccupied with the twins' normal infant demands and is unaware she is getting so overwhelmed that her attention to Lee has changed dramatically. She needed her husband to point out that Lee was spending a great deal of time alone after school. He comes home to find

Lee in his room, curled up in bed watching TV while his mother is in the babies' room coddling them, perhaps overprotectively because she so enjoys being close with her little ones. When he asks Lee the shows he's watched, he realizes he's been watching them for at least two hours by himself after school. He'd dutifully done his minimal amount of homework by himself and then spent his time staring at the TV screen.

When Lee's mother calls him down to dinner, Lee yells, "No. I'm not hungry." In reality, he *is* hungry, having only had a small snack after school, and his mother knows this. She yells upstairs a few more times and gets the same response. When Lee's dad goes upstairs instead of yelling from the first floor, Lee hugs his father and asks to be carried downstairs. His naysaying stops immediately when he has this comforting attention. This scene repeats itself often in their home.

One evening, Lee's mother complains to Lee's father that Lee has been saying "No" all day to what she believes are small requests, such as getting a blanket for one of the twins, playing with one brother while she changes the diaper of the other, and putting his snack plate in the sink after school. "And now that the twins are more active," she says, "when they knock Lee's toys down by mistake, Lee becomes aggravated and yells at *me* for not watching his brothers do these things to him." She feels helpless.

The next day, when Lee yells at one of the twins for messing up his toys, his mother scolds him for raising his voice to a baby when he is the bigger brother. Further, she asks him to pick up his toys since his brothers are too little to do so. In response, Lee shouts, "No. No. I hate them, and I hate you! You clean them up." Even when Lee makes a mess of his toys by himself and is later told to put them away, he says "No." Then he lies and blames one of his younger brothers and says they made the mess. It's not uncommon for a six-year-old not to clean up his toys or even to jealously blame his younger siblings, but Lee does this repeatedly and acrimoniously. Sometimes, he makes things even messier just to spite his mother because he feels so angry at her.

Lee's father points out to his wife that Lee's general low toleration for frustration has increased exponentially over the past six months, and they have to use their Parental Intelligence if they don't want his oppositional behavior to escalate further. Reluctant—because deep down she feels guilty for neglecting Lee—she agrees they have to step back and face the situation.

They review when Lee is in his angry moods, says "No" to his mother's requests, and spitefully aggravates her. Lee's father suggests his wife open her mind a bit more to Lee's naysaying because perhaps it's actually a way to assert himself about something they have yet to understand.

Lee's father goes even further. He says, "Saying 'No' can seem so negative that we might actually miss the importance of his words. Expressing himself by saying 'No' may be unexpectedly growth-promoting because he is trying to articulate something he's going through. What I mean is that he's inviting us to listen to something that's really bothering him, and we need to listen carefully. You've always been such an understanding mother. I wonder if something is blinding you to understanding him from that perspective. Sweetheart, we need to think this through."

Self-reflecting, she admits, as a twin herself, she seemed to identify more with her baby boys than with Lee, and this could be interfering with her good judgment. Her husband compliments her for this insight and suggests they recognize Lee's behavior is outside the norm for a six-year-old, even with twin siblings.

Lee's mother had been favoring the twins, and she had to face the inevitability of her ways. She adored taking care of babies, and Lee's growing up had actually felt like a loss. His becoming such a good student had not been regarded by her as positively as Lee needed and had earned because she felt his independence from her as losing their earlier mother-baby bond.

Together, Lee's parents now see the obvious. Lee is jealous of his mother's attention to the twins, and she has not adequately noticed and validated his six-year-old needs for attention and approval. Especially when she asks him to help with the twins, he becomes aggravated. They decide to hire a babysitter to come over and play with the twins when Lee comes home from school so he can have her undivided attention for about two hours. This problem solving is immediately effective. Lee calms down, stops storming about, and is no longer spiteful toward his mother. He appreciates her approval of his well done homework, and they share some conversations about school so he really feels cared for and heard. He even starts helping with the twins after his two hours alone with his mother.

Lee didn't resent the twin boys as much as he resented his mother's dismissal of him. When that was solved, his opposition eased and stopped. Indeed, his saying "No" so often was a way for this young boy to assert himself about what was troubling him. Problem solving with Parental Intelligence saved these busy parents much heartache and supported their oldest son's adjustment to his new siblings.

TIPS FOR PARENTS WHOSE CHILDREN SAY "NO" TOO FREQUENTLY

1. Step back and recount when and where the naysaying behavior occurs.

2. Notice if the opposition is occurring in more than one venue, such as school and home.

3. Self-reflect on the anger your child is showing, and see if it reminds you of any anger you may have had toward others in the past. Also consider if your child's anger reminds you of anger toward you from the past from someone important to you. In other words, consider how your past might be affecting your present parenting judgment.

4. Ponder carefully about what's to be expected at your child's developmental age. Think about his general temperament prior to the oppositional behavior, see if it has changed, and question why.

5. Pulling all the clues together, look for underlying reasons for the negative behavior. Focusing on what your child is saying "No" to might be a major piece of the puzzle. Once you understand how your child's mind is working, you can set about problem solving to meet your and your child's needs.

Evie has always been a strong-willed child. She was a determined toddler, a stubborn elementary school child, and a vigorously strong-minded tween. But she hits her stride as a teenager. By seventeen, she is self-centered and totally focused on getting her driver's license and performing well in school to get into a good college. Despite her mother's insistence, Evie refuses to complete normal household chores, eat her mother's meals, or listen to her mother's advice about clothes. She becomes fiercely independent, shifts to a strictly vegetarian diet, colors her hair orange, and wears too-revealing blouses and short, tight skirts. She and her mother battle constantly, more than in the average mother–teenage daughter relationship.

Evie's mother considers herself an easygoing, though busy, single, working mother. Because she has only one child, she feels she balances work and home life, and accepts that she and her daughter have different temperaments. For the most part, she actually admires her daughter's strong will and assertive style and even envies it a bit. But now she fears for Evie's judgment. Being a vegetarian can be healthy, but it means her mother needs to learn a new cooking style. Even though this is demanding, it is adventurous, and she accepts it. But orange hair and seductive clothes are beyond her ken. She has to object for Evie's sake because she fears Evie will become sexually active when she is too young to handle the potential consequences. Any attempts she makes to curb these excesses are met with adamant naysaying by Evie.

In effect, Evie's mother is forced to step back because Evie resists any discussions. She has watched the pattern of her burgeoning independence since Evie was little and isn't really surprised that her wish for autonomy grew when she became an adolescent. But she can't account for Evie's poor judgment. That is new.

Self-reflecting, Evie's mother remembers Evie had once been an agreeable only child to two parents in an initially intact family. But, when she divorced Evie's drug-addicted father when Evie was three, it had been very difficult for both mother and daughter. In fact, this family was intact only briefly because of the father's addiction. Evie couldn't possibly understand her father was sick and boldly indifferent to raising their child. He was in and out of rehab for most of her first three years and had no real relationship with Evie. She would only see him periodically, and they didn't develop a connection. After the divorce, he had moved constantly and no one currently knew his whereabouts. This saddened Evie's mother because she couldn't give Evie more knowledge about her father and didn't know the impact that loss would have on Evie now that she was old enough to see others on drugs. Evie was aware her father had a drug addiction, but not much more because he had basically vanished from their lives. Because Evie's mother had married young, rather impulsively infatuated with her husband who was her first and only boyfriend, she was afraid that Evie, too, could get caught up in a social life that was unguided and impetuous.

Developmentally, Evie's clothes and hair are outside the norm of her close friends, and she is becoming isolated from them and veering toward a more fast-moving circle of kids. Academically, Evie is different from these edgier teens, but socially she is drawn to their sexual and drug experimentation. Evie's mother realizes she knows very little about Evie's social life because she is busy at work and tired when she gets home, and Evie is so independent she doesn't draw her mother into conversations about her life. Facing all this, she realizes she has to understand her daughter's mind and that conversations are needed. But how should she approach her?

Evie's mother decides that Evie understands honesty and forthrightness, no pussyfooting around. She confronts her one Saturday afternoon after Evie tells her she is going out that night but not when, where, or with whom.

"Evie. We barely talk. I know you like to be on your own, and I admire that, but I'm worried about you. You always seem mad at me for having opinions different than yours. I know you realize people have different perspectives, so I don't understand why you're so infuriated with me when I express my point of view. We can disagree. We always have on many things. But now you seem angry all the time at me. Please, let's talk openly about what's on your mind these days. I promise not to judge you or blame you for any choices you are making. I just want to understand."

"I don't know if you really can understand me. Would it surprise you to know that I'm curious about kids who like drugs? We never discuss my father, but he had or has an addiction. We don't even know where he is. I'm trying to understand what that's all about, so I'm hanging out with kids who experiment. I haven't used drugs at all, but I'll admit I have been at parties where kids smoke pot, and I don't know what else they are actually doing. Dressing as I am helps me fit in with them, as if I belong."

"That's quite a burden you are carrying. I'm so proud of you for telling me what's been troubling you. Are you comfortable with your new hair color and clothes?"

"Kind of not. But if I don't look like I belong, then they won't invite me to their parties. I know I seem angry probably all the time, but it's a bit of a cover for how tough I want to be."

"Do you think that since you were young after my divorce, your stubbornness and saying 'No' to me so much was also a cover for how tough you thought you had to be without having a father that you knew or even understood? Am I on the right track?"

"I never saw it like that before, but maybe there's something to it. I think I need to go to a therapist with you to figure more of this out. Lots of kids I know see therapists and are really open about it. So maybe it's time for us to think about it, too. I'll admit, I'm scared about the decisions I'm making and how angry I feel all the time. I'm angry sometimes that you didn't help my father more. But I don't know if that's fair. I'm angry at him even though I don't know him because he really left me—left us—without any ways to reach or connect with him. Maybe a therapist could help us untangle this mess. Would you do that with me? I know how busy you are, and I don't tell you, but I appreciate how hard you are trying to be a good mother—even learning how to cook like a vegetarian!"

"Of course, I'm very willing for us to get professional help. Let me look into finding a really good person for us to be guided by. Okay?"

"You think I'm tough, but really you are the strong one. Mommy, this is our chance to get to know each other better. I do want to rely on you. I have no one to talk to. I think it's time you tell me more about my father."

Evie's mother holds back her tears when her daughter calls her "Mommy." She is reminded that Evie is still just a little girl, suffering inside with a brittle outer shell. She can tell Evie needs her and loves her. She is deeply proud of Evie for being so open.

TIPS FOR PARENTS WHOSE TEENAGERS SAY "NO" TOO FREQUENTLY

1. Keep an open mind about the meanings behind defiant behavior.
2. Think of the opposition as a communication that needs to be articulated and understood. Your teen is not "bad" but rather distressed, and her behavior is an invitation for you to understand her better.
3. Retain a non-blaming, non-judgmental attitude if you hope to learn what is on your teenager's mind.
4. Reach out to your adolescent even if she seems reluctant to talk. Showing you want to talk and care to listen to what may frighten you demonstrates the love you feel, and you may be surprised when your teenager actually discloses her feelings and thoughts.

5. The key to finding out what underlies the angry feelings is asking questions and offering insights, even if they are dismissed. When your ideas are dismissed, it doesn't mean your teen didn't hear and think about them. Have patience.

6. This may seem like a long process, but if you are actually open to your teenager's thoughts, feelings, and beliefs, you will more quickly understand her intentions than if you jump to conclusions and impose hasty consequences for behavior you don't understand. How can you know what to do if you don't understand first what you and your teen are experiencing? Understanding before acting indeed saves busy parents a lot of time.

In the short and long run, finding out the meaning behind defiant behavior with children and teens leads you in the direction of solving the problems that lie behind expressions of anger. This not only resolves the pain of feeling angry, but also strengthens the parent-child and parent-teen bond. Remember that bearing angry feelings is indeed painful and needn't be combative, but instead can be a pathway toward deeper understanding and problem resolution—ultimately what busy, caring parents and their kids yearn for.

Also, remember that when kids say "No" and oppose your requests, this may be a means of demonstrating they can think for themselves and have their own opinions and viewpoints. Saying "No" symbolizes a wish for more autonomy from grownups and shouldn't always be viewed as an undesirable response. In fact, it is quite often a marker of growth in that the child seeks more independent thinking and self assertion. This is a positive mark of development. Like most parents, you feel responsible to help your child or teen find constructive avenues to manage and handle his or her anger. But later, you need to feel confident that your child can control his or her anger on their own. If you think of this as your child's job, though he or she may need your help, it gives perspective to the weight of the responsibility you may feel. Solid positive self-esteem depends on the child's and teen's inner awareness of being able to control their angry feelings; as parents, we want to give our kids this sense of inner security and pride in their ability to accomplish controlling their emotions on their own.

CHAPTER FOUR

WHEN PARENTS SAY "NO"

I don't know how often I've heard parents complain that their kids don't listen to them when they say "No." It's a common cry for help from well-meaning parents who are just trying to set reasonable limits for their kids. Saying "No" is part of life with regard to requests for material things, and an attempt to teach responsibility about what things cost, what should be prioritized, and how to tolerate frustration when a child can't always have what they want in general.

Kids' and parents' days are filled with schedules, so it's simply not feasible to say "Yes" to every request for a playdate, an after-school activity, or a sleepover. The more kids in a family, the more complicated it gets—especially for busy working parents. Kids compete for their parents' attention and can be quite self-centered, so they sometimes barely give a thought to why the parent says "No," "Not now," or "Not today."

Seven-year-old Deirdre has an obstinate streak. The middle kid of seven children, she never feels she gets her fair share of anything. When one parent says "No" to any request, she runs to the other. The parents know this pattern and try to be consistent. One day, she asks to go to two different parties on the following Saturday. She wants to feel included in both groups of girls and wants her mother or father to pick her up halfway through the first party to attend the second. But seven siblings means seven different schedules, and it's impossible. Deirdre cries bitterly and angrily that her parents don't see her point.

Stepping back and using Parental Intelligence, her mother doesn't get into a big debate, but instead asks her more about the different groups of girls. Deirdre explains that she wants to fit in with the popular group (the first party), but her closest friends (the second party) are actually more fun, and she doesn't want to have them think she doesn't care about them. "You just can't say 'No' to me all the time. I hate it when you do that. Why don't you listen to me? You only want me to listen to you!"

Self-reflecting is tough for Deirdre's busy mother, who wanted a big family but now surely sees the complexities of satisfying everyone.

Her husband at first thinks his wife self-reflects too much and should just let "No" mean "No." "This is ridiculous," he says. "Teach her instead about why being popular isn't so important and that she should be loyal to her closest friends." However, he has second thoughts about what he says and realizes he and his wife do need to understand what "No" means to Deirdre. Deeply believing in the use of Parental Intelligence, he realized they had to be "meaning-makers" together. He felt he reacted too quickly to his wife and agreed they should try and help Deirdre figure out the meaning of popularity, how she can understand when she can't have what she wants at the moment, and what's really going on in her mind.

While her parents are stepping back, Deirdre has time to tolerate the frustration she is pretty used to and asks her oldest brother if he will pick her up from the first party and take her to the second. He understands her wishes and is available to do it. Deirdre's parents agree that would solve the immediate problem, but her father still wants Deirdre to contemplate this idea about being "popular," as well as understanding that she sometimes has to compromise about what she wants because she's part of such a large family.

"Deirdre, it seems you solved the problem on your own because your brother is so good to you. But can you think about the reasons why you care about being popular when you have such loyal close friends already?"

"Daddy, I'm not pretty like those popular girls. I was amazed the birthday girl even invited me. I think she did because I help her with her homework. So, this is a chance to see what it's like to hang out with other kids. How can I make choices about my friends if I don't even get to know these other girls?"

"Sweetheart, being the prettiest isn't as important as being the kindest, plus you are pretty, so I don't really get that. But you do have a point that it's good to stretch out who you know so you can make choices. Do you understand though why Mommy and I said 'No'?"

"Yes. I guess. You are really busy. You can't just cart the baby around wherever the rest of us want to go. I know that, but it bugs me. I want to listen to you, but I also want to you to listen to me! Get it?"

"Your thoughts are important, and Mommy and I are going to try to find the time to listen to you more. Is that what you are getting at?"

"You do get it. Thanks."

So Deirdre solved the initial problem in a short amount of time and also learned some lessons from her dad. Parental Intelligence prevented angry words going back and forth and even promoted sibling cooperation. Resisting a parent saying "No" was no longer the only issue because Deirdre did understand she had to have regard for others' needs in the family. Helping Deirdre understand the reasons behind the "No" was just as important as the meanings behind the reasons for her initial request. Thus, her parents were able to address the underlying problem about her need to feel heard, as well as provide her with further insight about the actual importance of popularity, a complex subject for a child to grasp. A major coup in a short amount of time with the help of Parental Intelligence!

TIPS FOR PARENTS SAYING "NO" TO CHILDREN

1. Consult with your parenting partner about the rules you want to set for your kids with regard to spending, chores, homework, curfews, and going to activities.

2. If you are a single parent, consider such rules on your own and try discussing these with other parents to get a sense of the norm in

your neighborhood. Hold fast to your own opinions even if you disagree with others. You need to set up your own values.

3. Instead of debating about your naysaying, listen attentively to what your child objects to. You may find there are underlying issues that can be addressed without arguing the initial "No."

4. It helps kids to know why you say "No." Sharing the fact that you are busy but care to listen is imperative if you want to understand your child's mind. If you need to say, "No. I can't talk now because we're in a store, but you can't have both toys," also say, "But, let's discuss it privately later." If you follow through, the next time a similar situation arises, your child will believe you and be more inclined to tolerate the "No" the first time it's said.

5. Understand the importance of limit setting; this will help you stick to your resolve. Limit setting helps kids tolerate frustration, consider others' needs and feelings, and learn to make good choices. These are essential life skills that parents want to impart. If you are having collaborative discussions, kids start to tolerate the "No's" because they, too, feel heard.

Ed and his father have been at loggerheads ever since Ed entered middle school. Now fourteen and entering high school, Ed is impossible to deal with any time his father says "No" to him. It can be about when his father is saying "No" he can't skip his shower and deodorant, "No" he can't be watching videos online instead of doing homework, or "No" he can't avoid his chores. Ed's father doesn't want to set up unreasonable consequences or threaten his son by saying, "No movies until you shower first," but he's at a loss how to appropriately and sensibly deal with these issues. Ed just doesn't want to hear his father's commandments. He argues, screams, and battles every "No" until his father feels like giving in or taking something away, which he knows only produces more resentment without any resolution that can build their relationship.

Stepping back, Ed's father thinks about being fourteen. He realizes Ed is going through puberty like wildfire. He'd grown two inches in the last year and was becoming quite muscular, his voice pitch had changed dramatically, and his body image was on his mind. As a father, he wasn't really prepared for all these changes and wondered if his son was prepared for his new body image. He has to admit he doesn't know his son very well anymore.

Self-reflecting, he knows he and his own father also had troubles at this stage. His father had been very authoritarian, and he didn't want to be that way, but yet he knew his requests and demands were on the mark. He winced at the idea of Ed not using deodorant, for example, and skipping showers. Didn't Ed know other people would realize it?

He understands Ed's development is normal but doesn't know what is on his mind that makes him so obstinate all the time. He guesses Ed maybe isn't really in tune with his bodily changes and, at the same time, wishes for more independence, but he doesn't know how to talk about all that. Rather than wait for a specific debate, he decides to approach his son at a quiet time when neither is rattled.

One Sunday afternoon, Dad asks Ed to watch a basketball game with him. Ed is up for that, so they put on ESPN, bemoan the bad calls, and talk about the players. During the commercial breaks, Dad gradually ventures to discuss more personal matters.

"Ed, I'm enjoying this game. Maybe we should get tickets to one during the season and go together."

"Yeah, Dad. I'd definitely want to do that."

"I know you are proud to be on the basketball team at school. I enjoy your games. What's it like in the locker room? Do the guys get along?"

"Yeah, pretty much. There's a lot of joking around about stuff, but I manage to keep up."

"I remember, when you tried ice hockey, the guys competed about how strong they were. It was awkward, I thought, at the time. Especially when you were on the travel team, I know you worried about all the competitive talk in the hotel rooms. Do basketball players have those kinds of talks?"

"It's kind of embarrassing, but yeah. I'm pretty big, so no one bothers me, but the skinnier guys get ribbed a lot. I try and stay out of all that."

"Do you feel when I remind you to take a shower and say that you can't skip it even one day, I'm kind of entering your private turf and I should back off?"

"Now that you mention it, it's weird actually. I'm a private guy, Dad. Maybe you think you're looking after me, but I've got a handle on how to take care of myself. When you tell me that kind of stuff, like the deodorant talks, I feel like running away from you. It's . . . well, sorry . . . but none of your business."

"I can see that. I'll back off. But just so you know, anytime you want to talk about this kind of stuff, I'm open and don't judge you. Really. I don't."

"Okay. The game's on now."

This was a meaningful talk for Ed and his father. They clarified the boundaries between them as father and son by discussing Ed's reactions to his father's naysaying. Ed's father could appreciate where Ed was coming from, and Ed actually shared quite a bit about sensitive bodily matters.

I suspect Ed now knew his father was onto his need for privacy and yet available for questions and problems should he have them. They are on the way to being more open and relaxed with each other. It can take time, but, for a busy dad, he certainly opened up a lot of doors.

TIPS FOR PARENTS SAYING "NO" TO TEENS

1. Notice if there is a pattern about what your teenager refuses to listen to when you say "No." Maybe there's a theme that has to do with the adolescent's stage of development.
2. Instead of arguing about the naysaying, try to open up a conversation about what bothers your teen about your saying "No."
3. Getting to know what's on adolescents' minds is difficult, especially when they are striving for independence and don't seek advice. But reaching out is accepted more easily than you might imagine if it's really clear that you're nonjudgmental and know when to back off from sensitive topics.

4. If it's a topic like homework and academics, sometimes it's important to have a discussion when homework isn't being done. Like Ed's dad, find a time when things are relatively laid-back and begin a discussion about future goals. Sometimes kids don't really think much about their futures unless parents broach the topic. Teens are living in the present, making plans at the last minute, and finding their way in social circles, so discussing the point of homework itself doesn't seem meaningful— just more school when they want a break. But if it's discussed in the context of learning with the purpose of planning one's career options, it may seem more important.

5. If you give advice about when to do homework and say something like, "No videos before homework," and your teen says, "I need a break now," listen carefully to him because he may have a good point, not just a means of defying your suggestion. (On the other hand, some kids are highly motivated and pressured to do extremely well academically with sights on exclusive colleges and difficult fields of study. These kids don't need prompting for their homework; in fact, it's sometimes helpful

to support them in taking some time off from the demands they put on themselves. This is why it's so essential to know your individual teen.)

6. Be conscious of how often you say "No" or set limits and whether it's essential. For example, some reliable kids don't need curfews. They find their own comfort in when their nighttime events should end. Other kids need the restrictions of curfews because they have trouble defining boundaries for themselves and even may silently like the limit setting. Again, know your individual teen.

Saying "No" and being listened to changes as kids grow up. But if you keep discussions and conversations open ended, you are less likely to get pushback at different ages. "No" is like a stop sign when you're driving; it's important to drive safely, but you don't always need a red light. Kids need to be able to deliberate and make good judgments. If you explain why you're saying "No" often enough, kids feel respected and are much more inclined to listen and think about your point of view.

CHAPTER FIVE

PARENTING THROUGH TEMPER TANTRUMS

*L*ara is a cheerful two-year-old who, like many kids her age, has trouble waiting for what she wants. Usually things stay in control when she and her parents talk things out, but when Lara went to Target with her father on Saturday, her impatience took a troubling turn. Just when Lara's father thought their shopping trip was over, Lara spies a yummy-looking chocolate bar at the checkout counter. "Ple-e-e-ase," she begs. But Dad says an emphatic "No." Lara lunges for it and then flops on the floor, crying, pleading, and screaming that she has to have it. The tantrum has begun. Dad knows he has to nip it in the bud, and with quick apologies to the checkout clerk, he picks up little Lara, and out the door they go. Shopping would have to wait for another day.

Eight-year-old Ward is upset. A child on the bus calls him "stupid." Ward prides himself on being smart. In fact, his intelligence boosts his otherwise delicate self-esteem. Ward isn't good at regulating his emotions, so he runs into the house screaming at his mother that he hates school. He lies on the floor, arms flailing, as he continues to yell about his day. He kicks his feet furiously. This lasts for ten minutes. Being called "stupid" erases all the praise Ward received from his teacher during the school day, and all those good feelings he had because of his teacher's positive words are lost. Ward's mother is beside herself even though she's seen this reaction many times. This is a typical temper tantrum for Ward after his feelings are hurt. Hours later, Ward's mother wants to discuss what happened, but all Ward can say is that he was called "stupid" and that it's really the other kid who "is dumb." Ward has mostly forgotten his tantrum.

WHAT IS A TANTRUM?

A tantrum occurs when a child's whole system of managing her feelings and thoughts collapses. A tantrum is a communication that seems to happen suddenly. The child may lay down on the floor and begin to scream. She will kick her feet on the floor, throw her arms about, and twist her body violently. Parents are usually so startled that they rush to pick up the child or hold them and check for bruises. As the parent becomes more frantic, so will the child. The suddenness and apparent lack of reason for the tantrums are always a shock to a parent who has not been through this before. It's hard to find the trigger and often it is a minor one, such as leaving a fun place, making a transition to a new activity, a prohibition, or a temporary frustration. It doesn't mean the parent is a bad parent or the child is a bad child. No one is bad. The child is desperately seeking some control over her body and pent up emotions, trying to find her own limits while expressing herself. The ultimate goal for the parent is to help the child learn what the tantrum means, as well as helping her find her own limits. It is an expression in external action of inner feelings over which the child is seeking control. The best thing you can do as a parent is learn to understand the reason for the tantrums and the propensity for them at different ages.

TEMPER TANTRUMS IN A CHILD MANAGED WITH PARENTAL INTELLIGENCE

After the age of three, most children can find some limits to their emotions without a tantrum, but let's look at ten-year-old Carrie, who has not mastered this self-regulation. Carrie has to decide what instrument to learn to play. Her music teacher gives her a choice of the violin or trumpet, two distinctly different instruments. Carrie feels upset and annoyed. For Carrie, this isn't a lovely opportunity to think for herself because decision-making has always been a vulnerability for her. She comes home from school triggered for a kind of breakdown that looks like anger has taken hold of her. First is the choice, then the build-up to making a decision which has been, for her, a gradual but increasing, thundering loss of control. She can barely give her mother the permission slip to sign with her decision.

It seems sudden to her mother, but actually it's been a growing, explosive discharge of tension: Carrie's skin turns red, her heart rate and breathing quicken, and her whole body flails and convulses on the floor as she cries uncontrollably. Her mother is flabbergasted, but glancing at the note, she realizes her daughter has been faced with a decision that will probably affect her for months to come and she must feel overwhelmed. She uses her

Parental Intelligence to quell this rising tide of excessive emotion in her sweet daughter.

Carrie can barely hear her mother's words as she steps back: "Carrie, let's take our time together. Let's slow down and see what has triggered this setback." Hearing her mother's calm voice slows Carrie down, even though she doesn't really hear the words. Carrie manages to get off the floor and sit up to the table where her mother had placed a snack before the tantrum began. She is trembling and can't possible even take a bite. Her mother reflects on how she, too, feels vulnerable when faced with a big decision, but this self-awareness makes her even more empathic and keeps her calm. She sits by Carrie, who is able now to let her mother put her arm around her. Knowing her daughter has a developmental delay in controlling her emotions when feeling stressed, she doesn't press her to make any decisions. They just sit together.

After ten minutes, Carrie's mother tells her that she is putting the permission slip away until later, and all Carrie needs to do now is eat her snack. A little food gives Carrie more energy and shifts her mood, so she is soon able to tell her mother what is on her mind. She explains that she likes her music teacher, and he trusts her to make up her own mind about which instrument to play. Now that she is calm, she remembers she can try each instrument with him to help her decide.

Her mother says, "So, you don't have to decide today, and I don't have to sign anything right away. Gee, you were so intent on making the choice, you forgot you don't have to act immediately, which is what angered and scared you."

Carrie is relieved as her mother reiterates the way to go about choosing is by trying to play each instrument a bit in school to see whether she wants a string or wind instrument.

This talk only took another ten minutes, but now mother and daughter are allies once again because the overstimulation of the decision-making has been relieved. The tantrum that looked like an angry explosion was really more about fear of making a wrong choice, and in the end they reached a positive resolution with Carrie's mother's help in shifting her daughter's perspective.

TIPS FOR PARENTS WHOSE CHILDREN EXPERIENCE TEMPER TANTRUMS

Strategies for coping with tantrums depend on the meaning behind the tantrum. Temper tantrums may look similar, but the reasons for them vary considerably.

1. A typical sign of a problem is when the child has trouble tolerating being told "No" in

response to something they want. This is often seen as the cause, but it's usually just the outward evidence of inner difficulties that need to be deciphered to know how to help the child. A tantrum which follows a parent or caregiver saying "No" is usually just the tip of the iceberg. Internal and external stressors prior to that have paved the way for the tantrum. Look for the meaning to the child behind the word "No."

2. Some children are very indecisive when given a single choice and they can become confused or upset about what to choose, for example, when they are told they can choose *one* toy in a store or *one* dessert in a restaurant. If a tantrum occurs in a situation where a child has to choose *one* activity or item, if the child is young, make the choice for the child in the immediate situation if necessary and empathize with the difficulty they had in making a decision. If the child is a bit older, tell them to delay making the decision until you've had a chance to talk it over together.

3. Some children become more vulnerable to frustration and even anger when there are family stressors, such as parents arguing or a

pending divorce. If a tantrum occurs after a family stressor, such as an argument between parents, calm yourself first. Next, do a quiet activity with your child, like reading a story. Then ask the child about her feelings when she saw or heard that her parents were mad at each other and listen patiently to her reply.

4. Siblings can become competitive, argue, then tantrum when they feel they are the loser in a fight for a toy or a parent's attention. Again, remaining calm is the key. Don't get into a debate about who gets what. Instead, separate the children and give them each something new to do. Later, have a discussion about how to take turns. Remember to initiate the discussion when everyone is calm.

5. Some children have sensory processing issues. That is, they have trouble taking in and understanding information. When they become confused, they can have temper tantrums. Make sure when you give an instruction, you make eye contact with the child. Make your requests simple and deliver them one at a time.

6. Some children are hypersensitive to touch, sound, and sight or have motor difficulties. They can fall apart when they're

overstimulated. Overstimulation can lead to tantrums. Children who like to be touched can be calmed with a hug. A hug can help them contain their emotions by giving them the attention they need and holding their body still.

7. Children who have difficulty with unexpected or planned transitions between activities may tantrum at those times or immediately afterward. You can prepare a younger child for a planned transition by advising them there are five minutes left before the change. You can give an older child an idea of the sequence of activities for the day so they feel prepared for what's ahead.

8. When the tantrum behavior slips outside the home, embarrassment becomes a new part of the equation. You may need to take faster action to help your child to prevent humiliation for both you and your child. If possible, attend quickly to what the child needs or remove the child from the situation, get back in the car to calm down, or go home if you need to. Leaving a public place is not a way to punish the parent or child, though it may feel that way. It's a way to quickly reduce the

stimulation and stop the outburst. When everyone is calm, perhaps even hours later, the parent can speak to the child about the situation. If the child is very young, their attention span is likely to be short, but a quick description of the problem along with a simple and easy rule like this can work: "Being upset belongs at home where we can solve problems." In this way, you can help your child to resume control of himself in the moment and the cause of the tantrum can be discussed when everyone is calm in the privacy of their home setting. In time, such a go-to rule about being upset at home, not in public, can be used automatically as needed. This becomes a self-regulating tool for the child, who internalizes this sentence eventually.

Claude is a seventeen-year-old who knows his laptop is filled with emails from the colleges he applied to, and there are bound to be some acceptances, some rejections. He is a good student and filled out the applications on his own with some editing help from his guidance counselor. He'd be loath to admit it, but he is actually set on two specific colleges that are his first choices. He's always been vulnerable to rejection because he works so hard at achieving his goals. He has also been a child who can't easily bear the frustration of not going where he wants to go. He's compensated well by hard work that usually leads him to achieve his expectations. However, he has an ambitious nature and angrily draws conclusions too quickly when he doesn't meet his goals at once. It takes him time to see from any perspective other than his own, which he holds all too strongly.

His mother asks if he wants her to be in the room when he opens the emails. He prefers to be alone and closes his door. He can't even sit at the computer when he opens the email. Standing, he reads he is rejected from three colleges that aren't important to him, but this sets him into a bit of a spin because they weren't that hard to get into, or so he'd thought. Then he is accepted to four more, which lifts his spirits, but he is still on edge. He's applied to fifteen colleges because he was so nervous about the outcome. The next two emails are from his favored schools. He finally sits down because he is trembling. Both schools have rejected him. At this point, he can't look further and has forgotten the great schools that accepted him. He screams at the top of his lungs, "I'm such a failure!"

His mother has stepped back during this process, feeling her son's tension, but at this point she knows she must enter his room before he has a total meltdown. He's already started throwing books around and has lifted his laptop off the desk. Seeing he might throw it with this as-yet-unarticulated rage, his mother says quietly but firmly, "Put the computer down and tell me what's happening." He only tells her about the rejections, but she knows he couldn't have possibly been rejected from all fifteen schools. She asks, "Do you want to take a break and slow this all down, or do you actually want to check the other schools? You are getting out of control and probably drawing erroneous conclusions about your future. What do you think?" She asks Claude what he thinks so he will start using his cognitive abilities instead of just acting out his emotions. Developmentally, he is acting like a younger child in this explosive way, and she is trying to help him prevent further regression in his emotional regulation. Faced with this situation, this mother is using her Parental Intelligence very wisely. She knows her son and is aware of what will slow down his reactions.

Claude cries inconsolably at first, still forgetting about the schools he was accepted by. At least his physical reactions turned into tears, a step forward. Finally, he controls himself more fully and admits his favored schools rejected him. This is a good sign because he is speaking now of what is actually on his mind that has upset him. Verbalizing what has upset him is the beginning of gaining much more control, which he is absolutely capable of at his developmental stage. Although the rejections seemed like a major setback to him, he is starting to think things through.

His mother clarifies: "They rejected your applications, not you as a person. You are not a reject or a failure."

Stunned by that comment, his sobbing stops and he looks her in the eye. "I never saw it that way before. It felt like each school was evaluating me as a whole person." To Claude's credit and renewed emotional stability, he is able to listen to reason.

His mother says, "You are the same intelligent, accomplished person you were before you opened those emails."

At that, he looks over the rest of the emails and finds he was accepted to the remaining colleges. While not overjoyed, he is indeed relieved and feels his mother is on his side. They decide to visit the top three schools he is interested in so he can make an informed decision based on his career goals.

So, once again, a busy mother using Parental Intelligence with her equally busy kid come to grips with reality, forestalling a potentially unnecessary huge tantrum.

TIPS FOR PARENTS WHOSE TEENS EXPERIENCE TEMPER TANTRUMS

When tantrums are viewed as meaningful, they become catalysts for change. Tantrum prevention requires careful observation of warning signs that most parents have learned by the time their kids are adolescents. They see when their teen is beginning to lose control—his voice is pitched higher, he may stumble over words, his face may redden, the muscles in his neck may stand out, and he may begin to throw things as he breathes faster.

1. First, make sure both you and your teen consider what's going on in his mind instead of focusing only on behavior. Internal and external stressors are identified so they can be addressed and alleviated.

2. Tell your teen that you and he can learn from this upset for the future. This can create a path toward ongoing creative problem-solving.

3. Once your teen has calmed down, use open dialogue to put a stop to disorganized reactions. Words replace physical actions. Once you help your child continue to talk about what's upsetting him, you will notice his whole body and mind settle down.

What seems bleak at first can lead to new understandings, new solutions to problems, and a stronger parent-teen relationship.

WHEN TO SEEK PROFESSIONAL HELP

Tantrums that last more than half an hour and are unusually intense with flailing limbs and shocking shrieks where the child or teen seems to be unaware of the world around her may end in the youngster being exhausted, falling asleep, and later not remembering the tantrum. These actions and emotions, especially in children four years and older, are not typical and need special attention. Tantrums can feel like panic attacks (see Chapter 3 of *The Busy Parent's Guide to Managing Anxiety in Children and Teens: A Parental Intelligence Approach*). They can be very frightening and overwhelming. It's important not to delay in getting professional guidance before they spiral or become a way of life.

Children and teens need to know their tantrums are not so powerful and scary that you can't tolerate them or stand up to them. The parent's role is to have the courage to use Parental Intelligence and tolerate the anger while looking out for your child or teen when he can't. In effect, you protect him from himself. With empathy, you share with your youngster that although he can't have what he wants, you understand why he feels so upset. The child or teen is less afraid of their emotions when they feel they can be understood and accepted. Seeing the parent stay in control is a model of emotional self-regulation that the child or teen eventually internalizes and uses in the future.

Kids with ADHD, learning disabilities, or sensory problems are dealing with additional frustration compared to a more typical child or teen, so they might be more likely to have tantrums. Similarly, kids with anxiety, phobias, depression, experiences of traumatic events, or a tendency to feel overstimulated may fall apart when they are overwhelmed with excessive worries and fears. A psychiatric evaluation and a psychopharmacological appraisal would be in order.

Some kids who have tantrums, particularly later in life but uncommonly when they are younger, may have a neurological disorder such as a bipolar disorder. Certain uncommon neurological problems can cause sudden violent outbursts. Thus, a neurological evaluation might be called for in addition to a psychiatric assessment.

It is apparent that tantrums range on a very broad continuum from a small skirmish for a three-year-old to a more intense meltdown by a teen. Only when tantrums are recurrent during the child's growing up years does professional help become warranted. When in doubt, always seek a consultation with a professional specializing in mental health for children or teens. The consult can be reassuring that this is a temporary setback or a sign of something more significant. As parents, the best we can do in the moment is to remain calm ourselves. In the long run, it is important to become as knowledgeable as possible about what is on our child's mind so we can understand the behavior and then know how to address it.

CHAPTER SIX

ANGER RESULTING FROM INTERPERSONAL SITUATIONS

Sometimes anger seems to come out of nowhere. Kids seem disgruntled, on edge, and snap at almost everything. Often enough, it's a brief reaction to not getting what they want exactly when they want it, earning a low grade at school on an assignment, or other fleeting happenings in daily life. However, other times, using Parental Intelligence, we learn there are deeper underlying reasons for this anger, such as an interpersonal rejection. This may be perceived or real, but to the child or teen it is very real. Their social lives are integral to their development, especially beginning in elementary school and most assuredly in the upper grades. In addition, perceived or real rejection from parents can weigh heavily on a child or teen's mind.

Carl is entering kindergarten. He is a generally cheerful child with lots of spunk and energy. He lives with his parents and grandmother, whom he loves dearly. His father has some difficulty understanding the normal development of a five-year-old and often expects him to conform to more adult standards of behavior than is reasonable. If Carl forgets to brush his teeth or leaves the sink a mess and whines when his father tells him harshly to straighten the bathroom up and listen, his father gets angrier than the circumstance warrants and Carl cries miserably. He fears his father at those times.

Carl's mother, on the other hand, is softer and more adept at understanding developmental stages. She and her husband have many discussions about what their expectations should be for their delightful son. Sometimes, although the discussions are in low tones, the father leaves the house to cool off. He slams the front door angrily and doesn't come back home until after Carl is asleep, so Carl doesn't know his father returned. Both parents work, so Carl's grandmother cares for him during the day. His father travels for his work, so again, Carl isn't always aware of where his father is.

Finances are tight, so Carl didn't attend preschool, but he went to the library and other town activities for preschoolers before attending kindergarten. Still, he hasn't socialized as often as most of the kids entering school that year. True to his nature, however, he is optimistic about kindergarten, visits the school a few times during the summer with his mother or grandmother, and looks forward to feeling like a big boy on a school bus.

After about a month of school, Carl's mother is shocked to learn that her normally well-behaved son is disruptive in class. She goes to the school conference alone because her husband is away on a job. This is a parent conference that kids do not attend. She is told that Carl is pinching the other kids and having several arguments with one particular boy that leads to pushing and shoving.

Furthermore, he seems to seek more attention from the teacher, Mr. Richards, than the other kids and always hugs him hello and goodbye whenever they see each other for the first and last time of the day and when they are not in the classroom at the same time. He hugs him when school begins and ends, before and after recess, and before and after he goes to the bathroom.

Mr. Richards suggests to the mother at the conference that Carl is insecure and fears rejection, not only by the other kids, but also by him, his teacher from whom he needs this constant physical reassurance with hugs.

Carl's mother shares the upsetting news from the teacher with Carl's father when he comes home. He was set on yelling at Carl for pinching when Carl's mother reminds him about stepping back and trying to figure all this out. Stepping back and self-reflecting are hard for this man who is quick to anger himself and usually believes in immediate consequences for actions. He needs his wife to remind him especially about stepping back and not rushing forward with instant reactions. With Carl's mother's encouragement to step back and with her loving help to self-reflect, he slowly and painfully remembers how his alcoholic father raged at him for the smallest misdeed and considers that he has a similar temper. He feels guilty about this and regrets his tendency to take after his own father. The parents decide to talk with Carl about the situation at school.

The mother begins, "Carl, your teacher says that you are upset at school and get angry and pinch. Also, that you need lots of hugs during the day. Can you tell us about this?"

"Wade is a mean boy. He chases me and pinches me, and I pinch him back. Mr. Richards blames me because I did it last, but it's not my fault. No one likes me because everyone likes Wade best."

Clearly, Carl feels this boy picks on him and makes it hard for him to make other friends. He feels rejected by the other kids and doesn't hold back his anger from his mother that no one likes him.

Carl's father asks why he needs so many hugs from the teacher. Carl says, "Because I want to make sure he won't leave me alone in the class with Wade. When I go to the bathroom, I'm afraid he won't be in the room when I come out. Mr. Richards thinks I'm bad, but I'm not. The other kids think I'm bad, too. I get checks on the blackboard next to my name for pinching. So everyone thinks I'm a terrible person and they don't like me. This makes me mad. It's not fair. I don't like being told off by Mr. Richards. When I hug him, he hugs me back, which makes me feel better. I tell him I love him and draw him a happy picture. Then I know he won't leave me."

Carl's parents are blown away by his honesty and fears of being rejected and left. It doesn't take them long to connect it to his father's leave-takings from the house when he was mad, compounded by his traveling for work. The pinching was an expression of anger that Carl had trouble expressing at home, so it came out at school. The other kids observed his actions and were staying away from Carl, so he felt rejected. Insightfully, Carl's father connects the comment about "being told off" with the fact that he also did that with Carl much too often for minor infractions of rules and routines. He feels badly about that.

In time, with the support of Carl's mother, Carl's father becomes less aggressive and develops a routine of always letting Carl know where he is going and when he'll return. This not only gives Carl the security he needs and lessens his anger, but also relieves the marital tensions that were another stressor for this little five-year-old. By summer camp and first grade, Carl's anger subsides and he makes friends, yet still needs the reassuring hugs.

More time is needed to heal all his fears, but a lot had been accomplished. Carl had felt rejected not only by other kids but also by his father. When Carl's parents were able to figure all that out, they could set out to solve the problems. Because of their efforts to understand the issues behind Carl's anger, Carl's anger was resolved. He behaved well and made friends at camp and in first grade.

TIPS FOR PARENTS WHOSE CHILDREN EXPERIENCE INTERPERSONAL REJECTION

1. Step back and look for clues of angry behavior in young kids that may be acted out in school and/or at home.

2. Self-reflect on one's own angry behaviors that may stem from earlier in your life that are still being acted out in the present, only now with your child.

3. Clarify developmental expectations so the child can meet your rules and routines successfully and garner your loving approval that is so needed by children from their parents.

4. Discuss the problems that surface even with young kids, who are often much more forthcoming than older kids. They tend to say what's on their minds in an unguarded fashion when they know no one is getting angry with them or blaming them.

5. Knowledge about where their parents are at all times is essential for young children. This secures their attachment and helps them overcome the normal separation anxiety that exists at early ages. (For more information about separation anxiety, go to Chapter 5 in *The*

*Busy Parent's Guide to Managing Anxiety in
Children and Teens: The Parental Intelligence
Way.*)

It is Saturday morning, and Leslie, a fit fifteen-year-old,
is hiding out in her room. Leslie's parents divorced when
she was six. Even though her father used to visit periodically for the first five years, she hasn't seen him much
lately and misses him terribly. At first, she had hoped she
would forge a closer connection with him as she grew
older, because in her mind he just wasn't good with little
kids. But then, when she was nine, he remarried and had
more kids with his new wife that kept him at an even
greater emotional distance. When she was eleven, he
moved what Leslie angrily called his "other family" across
the country. Their contacts were minimal, her anger
turned to despair, but her yearnings continued.

Alone in her room, Leslie slips in and out of sleep as
an all-too-familiar sadness sinks over her as she recalls
her last dance recital when she was fourteen. It was
the culmination of all her recitals because she was the
star of the show. It was a year ago, but it feels like no
time has passed. She knows her sadness is combined
with an anger that turns to fury, and sleep is her escape.
Awake, she remembers being at the theater wondering
if her father was in the audience as he'd promised. Even

though he had broken so many promises, she still had secretly sent him a letter inviting him to this special show where she was going to dance a solo accompanied only by a jazz quartet. He did respond, promising he'd be there.

Her anger peaks when she realizes over and over that he had never shown up; a heavy weight of disappointment just won't leave her. She falls back asleep.

Leslie's father's absence was such a rejection that she couldn't dance anymore. It was a brutal blow. She tried practicing after that last performance, but the weight of his betrayal kept returning, and she couldn't dance any more. His broken promise felt like a blatant lie. The only way to relieve herself of this violation was to give up dance. It worked for a while, but now, one year later, the weight returned and melancholy hung on beyond the initial anger.

As if that wasn't enough, her boyfriend of four months, Craig, had recently broken up with her. Leslie is angry that he got into drugs, which was not her thing, and that he was now seeing someone else. He was a good listener, though, and she misses him. He turned to drugs to escape like Leslie used sleep. She had told him about her father and was angry he knew her secrets and left her alone.

Leslie's mother, Ceci, notices how curt Leslie has become with her and has stopped her usual sharing of confidences. She feels like a bad mother; she feels she doesn't know her daughter anymore and doesn't know what is going on. She also feels this nagging hesitation to approach her daughter, which isn't like her usual manner. She feels herself resist self-reflection and blames it on being busy with her work, but deep inside she knows there is more to it than that.

Ceci broods about her lack of helping her daughter. As she passes Leslie's uncommonly messy room, she feels an inexplicable, uncharacteristic rage well up inside her, and the emotion surprises her. She thinks, *I have no idea how to handle the situation between Leslie and me. I'm so afraid she'll see my rage that I can't account for.* Ceci remembers how, at first, Leslie became really curt and stopped confiding in her. That was so unusual. Stepping back, she tries to remember when Leslie stopped talking to her.

Then as if out of the blue, she begins self-reflecting and finds herself thinking of her relationship with her own mother when she was Leslie's age. Leslie's detachment reminds Ceci of her mother's long bouts with clinical depression, a situation that used to make her very angry. At fifteen, Ceci was forced to take care of her nearly immobilized, weeping mother. She sat by her side for long periods of time, trying to comfort her to no avail. It kept her away from her adventurous friends, whom she envied. She suddenly realizes her own memories of her mother caused her present unaccountable rage to resurface. Wanting to forget this memory has blocked her from seeing Leslie might be depressed. First her mother, and now her daughter?

Holding on to a thought that tidy Leslie's surprisingly messy room might mirror her mental state leads her to another revelation: *I've been thinking so much about mothers that I've forgotten all about fathers. At least when I cared for my mother, my father was proud of me and thanked me. But Leslie doesn't have a father to boost her self-confidence. How could I have been so blind? How could she possibly cope with his absence, which is not only physical, but also emotional? The loss of my understanding only compounded the loss of his understanding. She must be feeling so alone and angry at both of us.*

With this insight, Ceci realizes, *Leslie can't straighten up her room because she can't think straight!* She goes to Leslie's room and, slowly but surely, her daughter pours out her anger and depressed feelings. She confesses to her mother about the recital, about feeling rejected by her girlfriends whom she'd lost contact with because she stopped responding to their invitations to do things, and even about Craig's rejection, as well.

Leslie says, "I was worried that if I told you how much I missed Daddy and needed a father now, you would feel like you'd let me down."

Ceci responds, "I'm glad we are able to talk together, and I have an idea that might help. Would you like me to talk to your father? It must have been difficult to communicate with him on your own all the time. I know he loves you. He just doesn't know how to show it."

"Yes," responds Leslie, feeling a great release of tension. "I would like you to do that for me."

There was something so caressing in their words as they leaned toward one another, giving Leslie hope. Her anger and despair drained out of her.

"Thank you for being so patient with me and understanding me, Mommy." Leslie had regained the faithful lifeline that her mother had always represented. In particular, Ceci felt she could now help her daughter deal with the problem presented by her absent father. Theirs was a unique bond. (For more detail about this story, read Chapter 10 of *Unlocking Parental Intelligence: Finding Meaning in Your Child's Behavior*.)

TIPS FOR PARENTS WHOSE TEENS EXPERIENCE INTERPERSONAL REJECTION

1. Step back and look for clues of angry behavior in teenagers that may be acted out in school and/or at home.

2. Self-reflect on one's own angry behaviors that may stem from earlier in your life that are still being acted out in the present, only now with your teen.

3. Reflect on how you may be blocking out your own anger from the past, which prevents you from seeing your teenager's anger and its causes.

4. Teens are capable of abstract thinking and gainfully accessing insight with their parents' help. Help them link the sources of their anger and how to understand and cope with their problems.

Interpersonal rejection can take different forms, including feelings of social and parental rejections. Busy parents can support their rejected child or teen with Parental Intelligence that brings the underlying issues to light so they can be problem solved effectively.

RESOLVING THE PARENT-CHILD ANGER SPIRAL AND DEEPENING THE PARENT-CHILD RELATIONSHIP

*A*ngry feelings over an impending or current experience are common for children and teens periodically. We have seen the wide variations in the manifestations of anger in children and teens that, with Parental Intelligence, busy parents can help their kids voice, modify, and remedy. It is a continuous process between parent and child or teen that results in an alliance that deepens their relationship. The parent who does not judge their angry child or blame them for their feelings becomes an ally that the child internalizes so he or she doesn't feel alone with these intense emotions.

It's important you see your child's or teen's anger as just a part of them, not the whole person. Angry expressions are just one emotion that your child has that may conceal other emotions, such as hurt and anxiety. (See *The Busy Parent's Guide to Managing Anxiety in Children and Teens: The Parental Intelligence Way.*) In addition, while children may show out-of-control anger often, they are likely also functioning well at other times with more control of their emotions. Your role is to help your child or teen recognize when they lose control as compared to other times when they feel more stable and able to regulate their feelings. You can help your sons and daughters recognize patterns of loss of control, so they can understand and anticipate when this may happen, learning coping strategies that forestall emotional dysregulation.

Although some degree of anger is commonplace, in that everyone experiences that emotion from time to time, there are many different potential causes and degrees of intensity at different developmental stages in children's and teens' lives. The impulse control of a two-year-old is clearly less than that of a ten-year-old. However, when puberty begins and teenage hormones surge forward, impulse control may again weaken, though not to the extent of the preschool child. Using Parental Intelligence, busy parents can help their child or teen with different levels of anger at these different stages of growth.

If you feel parental guidance is not sufficient and the anger is abnormal, don't be afraid to seek professional help. Neurological and psychiatric disorders may be involved, warranting an evaluation for psychotherapy and medications that can help your child relieve angry outbursts and more clearly define the causes of the intensity and frequency of these powerful emotions.

Although this book has focused on the anger in children and teens, it is also important to address angry feelings in the parent as well. Your past angry experiences can help you empathize with your child's or teen's emotions so, as their mother or father, you understand more fully what your child or teen is going through. On the other hand, your anger can exacerbate your youngster's angry state of mind and lead to unnecessary parent-child or teen power skirmishes that only divert the youngster from understanding the actual origins of their emotions. For example, yelling at your screaming youngster for their behavior only makes things worse, creating a new battle that results in additional squabbling and bickering that only exacerbates whatever was on the child's or teen's mind in the first place.

Parents suffer when their kids suffer. If your child's or teen's anger raises your own, then a spiral can begin where each person's tension increases the other's. An angry youngster needs a steady, stable parent to calm them down. This is done initially if the parent uses the first step of Parental Intelligence wisely, *stepping back*. If you react slowly and with ease to your child's edginess, taking the time to pause and consider the situation before bursting in with fast solutions, your child will sense your pace and slowly internalize it. Eventually, with your help, we hope children can learn to control their own anger by slowing down their motor, so to speak, to understand what they are experiencing enough to take some steps to modify their fury and come to grips with the causes of their state of mind.

If the parent-child anger spiral begins, it doesn't mean all is lost. You can still *step back* midstream, *self-reflect* (the second step of Parental Intelligence), and quickly consider what is promoting your own anger. When a parent is busy, this step is often left out, though in the long run, it saves time because self-understanding then leads to understanding your reactions to your child. Then you can *step back* once more and begin to *understand your child's or teen's mind* while also *understanding their stage of development*, the next steps in Parental Intelligence. If the busy parent has internalized this process, it will come naturally each time an issue with anger arises, and the child will incorporate the process, as well.

It needs to be reiterated that anger is a normal feeling in everyday life that is often warranted, and asserting one's thoughts is an important interpersonal skill. When you can model this ability to express yourself without losing control, your children observe and learn to manage their anger in a controlled way as well, learning to assert their beliefs, opinions, and points of view with vigor and self-confidence. In contrast, the family that denies the expression of such feelings may lead to an inhibited, restricted child who grows up believing their angry feelings are wrong and bad. This can lead to suppressed anger, instead of such feelings being directed at their source, leading to a depressed state of mind. Teach your children that anger is just one of a wide range of emotions they should feel free to express with due regard to the other person's feelings, thus learning empathy and supporting healthy development, a broad range of expression, and a feeling of positive self-worth. If you can foster this environment, you will find your parent-child relationship is strong and healthy and your youngster will learn to manage his or her anger naturally and maturely.

REFERENCES

Ekman, Paul. 2007. *Emotions Revealed: Recognizing Faces and Feelings to Improve Communication and Emotional Life.* New York, New York: Holt & Co.

Hollman, Laurie. 2015. *Unlocking Parental Intelligence: Finding Meaning in Your Child's Behavior.* Sanger, California: Familius.

Hollman, Laurie, 2018. *The Busy Parent's Guide to Managing Anxiety in Children and Teens: The Parental Intelligence Way.* Sanger, California: Familius.

ABOUT THE AUTHOR

LAURIE HOLLMAN, PhD, is a psychoanalyst with specialized clinical training in infant-parent, child, adolescent, and adult psychotherapy covering the lifespan. She is the author of the Gold Mom's Choice Award book, *Unlocking Parental Intelligence: Finding Meaning in Your Child's Behavior* and *The Busy Parent's Guide to Managing Anxiety in Children and Teens: The Parental Intelligence Way.*

Dr. Hollman has been on the faculties of New York University, The Society for Psychoanalytic Study and Research (of which she was president), Long Island University, and the Long Island Institute for Psychoanalysis.

She has written extensively for various publications on infant, child, and adolescent development, including the *Psychoanalytic Study of the Child, The International Journal of Infant Observation*, and *The Inner World of the Mother.* She has also written on subjects relevant to parents for the *Family Law Review*, a publication of the New York Bar Association. As a columnist for *Newsday's Parents & Children Magazine* and the *Long Island Parent* for almost a decade, she has also written numerous articles on parenting.

Dr. Hollman wrote the "Parental Intelligence" column for *Moms Magazine*, blogs for *Huffington Post*, and writes for *Thrive Global*. She has also been a feature writer for *Pittsburgh Parent, The Bay State Parent Magazine*, and *Active Family Magazine* and a guest writer for popular parenting websites, including *The Bloggy Moms Network, Natural Parents Network, Positive Parenting Ally, Our Parent Spot*, and *Parenting London Child*.

Dr. Hollman and her husband are the proud parents of two spirited, industrious, and loving sons.

ABOUT FAMILIUS

Visit Our Website: www.familius.com

Join Our Family

There are lots of ways to connect with us! Subscribe to our newsletters at www.familius.com to receive uplifting daily inspiration, essays from our Pater Familius, a free ebook every month, and the first word on special discounts and Familius news.

Get Bulk Discounts

If you feel a few friends and family might benefit from what you've read, let us know and we'll be happy to provide you with quantity discounts. Simply email us at orders@familius.com.

Connect

- Facebook: www.facebook.com/paterfamilius
- Twitter: @familiustalk, @paterfamilius1
- Pinterest: www.pinterest.com/familius
- Instagram: @familiustalk

The most important work you ever do will be within the walls of your own home.

CPSIA information can be obtained
at www.ICGtesting.com
Printed in the USA
FSHW01n1026180618
49434FS

9 781641 700115